strategies
for
freedom

# strategies
# for
# freedom

## the changing patterns of black protest

by BAYARD RUSTIN

columbia university press / new york / 1976

"If We Must Die" from *Selected Poems of Claude McKay;* copyright 1953 by Twayne Publishers, Inc. and reprinted with permission of Twayne Publishers, A Division of G. K. Hall & Co., Boston.

Library of Congress Cataloging in Publication Data

Rustin, Bayard, 1910–
    Strategies for freedom.

    Includes bibliographical references and index.
    1. Negroes—Civil rights.   2. Negroes—History
—1877–1964.   3. Negroes—History—1964–
I. Title.
E185.61.R967    323.4'0973    75-43598
ISBN 0-231-03943-3
Columbia University Press
New York    Guildford, Surrey
Copyright © Columbia University Press 1976
Printed in the United States of America

# the
# radner
# lectures

In 1956 the Radner Family Foundation established a lectureship at Columbia University in memory of William Radner, a graduate of Columbia College and The Columbia Law School. Since his career in the public service has been terminated by his untimely death, the gift appropriately stipulated that these lectures were to deal with subjects in the field of public law and government. Previous Radner Lectures were:

1959 Harry S Truman, Former President of the United States
"The Presidency"

1960 Lord Boothby, Rector of the University of St. Andrew's
"Parliament and the Profession of Politics in Britain"

1963 Robert R. Bowie, Director of the Center for International Affairs, and Dillon Professor of International

To A. Philip Randolph, whose integrity, wisdom, and courage have meant so much in the struggle for racial equality

The ideas presented in this volume are the product of three movements with which I have been fortunate to have been associated: the struggle for racial equality, the struggle for a better world for working people of the trade union movement, and the American social democratic movement. I could not, within the space of an entire book, give ample credit to the many individuals whose ideas and advice have contributed to my own thoughts on social struggle. I would, however, like to give special thanks to several people— friends and associates who have provided invaluable assistance in the development of ideas contained in this book.

dedication and acknowledgments viii

They include Tom Kahn, Rachelle Horowitz, Arch Pudding-
ton, Carl Gershman, and, particularly, Max Shachtman. I
am also indebted to Agnes McKirdy of Columbia University
Press for her valuable help in preparing the manuscript for
publication.

# contents

strategies
for
freedom

# 1
# the
# early
# years

The course of the Negro American's history during the twentieth century has been marked by a remarkable and unprecedented social transformation. For centuries blacks had been looked on by the larger society as sub-human entities—"Invisible Men." Brought here in bondage and abandoned with the end of Reconstruction, the Negro comprised the bottom layer of a caste system engraved into the public institutions and legal structure of the South. Discrimination was also rampant in the non-South, where blacks were excluded from the wealth of industrial America.

And yet blacks rose from oppression and discrimination to create the most dynamic social movement in American history. They have achieved through this movement a sense of dignity, a feeling of worth that derives from the ennobling nature of their struggle.

Once considered political nonentities, blacks have become a vital political force, whose special needs no politician can afford to disregard. And from an economic underclass—landless, poverty-stricken, consigned to menial, dead-end occupations— blacks have become participants in the mainstream of modern technological society.

The movement which enabled blacks to surmount the twin handicaps of racial and class discrimination was rooted in three basic principles: a belief that racial progress could only be achieved in an integrated framework, a commitment to the tactics of nonviolence, and a realization that broad, permanent change cannot be achieved by a movement confined to blacks—a belief, in other words, in coalition politics.

These three principles share one common theme, that of hopefulness. It is an important quality. For whenever blacks have adhered to integration, nonviolence, and coalition politics, they have succeeded in moving the man-made mountains of Jim Crow. They have removed racial barriers that had been carefully erected over the span of three centuries. They have won decisions from the courts, laws from the Congress, the support of presidents, and the encouragement of a majority of the American people.

It is true, of course, that integration has not always been the dominant philosophy within the Negro movement; long-simmering anger has boiled over into expressions of violence, and nationalism has had its day. Doctrines bred of frustration and hopelessness have marked the history of all social movements, particularly those confronted with seemingly insurmountable odds such as the ones blacks had to face. The point is that those periods which saw the rise of the ideologies of hopelessness were precisely the periods when past achievements were blunted, when a hard-won consensus of support was diminished, and when confusion, aimlessness, and disarray had replaced unity and purposefulness.

The contrasting careers of the two most prominent black radicals of the 1920s—Marcus Garvey and A. Philip Randolph—underscore this point.

One cannot argue with the proposition that Marcus Garvey was an important and influential figure. The mass movement he commanded, for a few stormy years, numbered in the hundreds of thousands. The more ardent of his followers embraced Garvey's doctrines of Pan-Africanism as a legitimate alternative to integration while others, caring little about the philosophical subtleties which separated Garvey from the majority of black intellectuals, entrusted him with their meager savings and then eagerly awaited the coming black capitalism bonanza which he had promised.

And yet, despite his widespread popularity, Garvey left hardly anything of permanence to the racial struggle. Today his career draws the notice of historians, but his ideas mean little indeed to the struggle of American blacks who, as every opinion poll demonstrates, continue to affirm the validity of integration. And as each passing year brings more progress for blacks within the context of American society, Garvey's nationalist ideas become less and less relevant.

Some would explain Garvey's eclipse as the result of financial bungling. Garvey the man failed, they say, but the philosophy he espoused contained merit.

Such an explanation is insufficient. Ultimately, Garvey failed because society judged his ideas impractical. Moreover, those blacks who were acquiring a sense of the shape of the coming struggle recognized that Garvey was not the revolutionary he claimed to be but rather a counterrevolutionary, more in the mold of Booker T. Washington. He was a thoroughgoing capitalist, and, in a sense, an accommodationist. Like Washington before him, Garvey rose to prominence at a time when it was becoming increasingly obvious that the rising expectations of Negroes were about to be shattered. For Washington, that time was the acknowledged end of Reconstruction, when the freedman was disenfranchised, deprived of his social and economic rights, and stripped of what he thought to be the legitimate legacy of emancipation. For Garvey, the time was the period immediately after World War I, when returning black troops discovered that making the world safe for democracy did not automatically signal the spread of democracy at home. And Garvey, like Washington before him, urged the Negro to cast down his bucket where he was. The Negro worker, he counseled, should "always keep his scale of wages a little lower than the whites until he is able to become, through proper leadership, his own employer."

It is ironic that A. Philip Randolph, perceiving in Garvey the makings of an incipient radical, should have provided Garvey with his first soapbox speaking opportunity in Harlem. The two were soon to become bitter antagonists, as Randolph's life took a sharply different turn.

Randolph did not move with the swiftness which marked Garvey's rise and fall. But his contributions were far-reaching and lasting. Where Garvey's social vision was narrow, Randolph's was total; he was always aware of the economic dimension of discrimination, and thus his various campaigns were directed at both class and racial bias. Randolph understood that for Negroes the arena of struggle was right here in the United States, and that the particulars of that struggle must be aimed at a massive restructuring of this nation's basic institutions, including a major redistribution of wealth.

Randolph also possessed a keen sense of strategy. It was this sense that set him apart from the rest of the black lead-

ership in those painful years when the nation began to hear
the first faint murmurings of the civil rights movement.

America heard those murmurings first in 1909, when the
Niagara Statement was issued, and then again, a little
louder, in 1910, when those who had prepared the Niagara
Statement formed the National Association for the Advancement of Colored People. Since its founding the
NAACP has served, often alone, as the pillar of black resistance. Its first broad program, drawn up in 1919, was the
cornerstone of the black agenda for decades to come. It
asked:

> The right of each qualified Negro man and
> woman to vote.
>
> The same access to an education that whites
> enjoyed.
>
> The right to a fair trial, presided over by
> judges whom blacks had a chance to help
> elect and a jury the members of which
> would be chosen without regard to a per-
> son's color.
>
> An end to "lynching and burning at the
> hands of mobs."
>
> Equal and integrated service on public
> transportation, integration of parks, li-
> braries and other public facilities, and equal
> job opportunities.
>
> The abolition of color-hyphenation and the
> substitution of straight Americanism.

This program addressed itself to basic principles of human dignity and constitutional rights. It did not encompass economic rights; this dimension was added later by A. Philip Randolph.

Nor did the NAACP's 1919 document deal with a strategic means for resolving discrimination. However, this lapse is in no sense a reflection on the NAACP. During those difficult years no one person or organization knew the means that would work to help blacks achieve equality. W. E. B. DuBois and Garvey thought they knew, but the course of history has demonstrated how deeply flawed their philosophies were.

The fact is that the racial caste system so pervaded American society in the early twentieth century that it had destroyed the potential for creative mass action and demoralized black leadership.

The American political process, which had provided some measure of hope for the burgeoning immigrant populations of the urban North, was foreclosed to black participation. Woodrow Wilson looked upon Negroes with an aristocratic disdain. Harding, Coolidge, and Hoover were suited neither by temperament nor philosophy to lend moral or political support to the oppressed. Even Franklin Roosevelt, the recipient, from 1936 on, of the overwhelming majority of the black vote, declined to throw the prestige of his office behind a piece of antilynching legislation, even though the bill had strong national support.

Nor could blacks appeal to the Supreme Court for redress. Republican appointees to that body gave it a visibly conservative tone. Not until midway through the 1940s did the influence of Roosevelt's appointments begin to make itself felt sufficiently to bring about a liberalization in the Court's racial outlook.

Shunned by the political parties, and rejected in the courts, blacks had to look outside the normal channels of democracy to press their cause. But even here the conditions of American society severely limited their options.

A protest movement of the scale mounted in the 1950s and 1960s was unthinkable during the early years of the century. Most Negroes lived in the rural South, where an effort to integrate public transportation, or sit in at a lunch counter would elicit immediate, and probably violent, reprisal. Some 277 lynchings were recorded between 1922 and 1934. In the South, membership in the Ku Klux Klan reached its peak during the 1920s, which was also the time when other protofascist organizations began systematically terrorizing blacks, Jews, and Catholics in the non-South.

The concerted efforts to destroy nascent radical movements in the United States—climaxed by Attorney General A. Mitchell Palmer's "Red Scare" of 1919—did not, except in a few instances, affect blacks directly. But they contributed to the atmosphere of repression and thereby disoriented those forces which might, under more tolerant circumstances, have served as valuable allies for blacks.

The radical parties displayed little understanding of the special problems confronting black Americans. The Socialist party, for instance, was strongly committed to ideal of racial equality, but failed to offer a platform directed at specific racial injustices. It did, however, have a program which, had it been implemented, would certainly have uplifted the condition of the black masses. That program was, of course, socialism—the overthrow of the capitalist system by democratic means and the institution of democratic control of the means of production and allocation of goods and resources. But the Socialist party had no racial platform. As its esteemed leader, Eugene V. Debs, explained: "We have nothing special to offer the Negro, and we cannot make special appeals to all the races." [1] As a longtime Socialist, and as national chairman of Social Democrats, U.S.A. (the party of Debs and Norman Thomas), I look upon the failure of the Socialists to make that special appeal as a tragic error. Because of the Socialist party's lack of foresight in this one respect, a generation of Negroes came and went, untouched by the doctrines of socialism, and unacquainted with its brilliant, visionary spokesmen. As a democratic organization, genuinely moved by human suffering, the Socialist party might have changed the whole course of the civil rights movement and hastened racial progress had its vision in the area of racial injustice been less narrow.

The other leading radical organization, the Communist party, went out of its way to enlist blacks, particularly black activists and intellectuals, into its ranks. But while the Communists had a larger black membership during this period than other left-wing groups, they too ultimately failed to appeal effectively to the black masses.

For one thing, the Communists were always viewed with suspicion as a potentially subversive group. Their leaders never had the respect that Debs or Norman Thomas achieved. As a people already stigmatized by the color of their skins, Negroes were not eager to further burden themselves with the notoriety of belonging to an organization

1. Jervis Anderson, *A. Philip Randolph: A Biographical Portrait* (New York: Harcourt, 1973), pp. 148–49.

many considered un-American. Furthermore, the Communists' position on the racial question—they favored the creation of a separate black nation carved out of several southern states—was utopian, hardly relevant to the Negro's day-to-day struggle for survival.

Finally, the Communist party failed to attract broad support in the black community for the same reason it failed to win permanent footholds in the labor movement, in the academic world, in politics, or in any of the other institutions it tried to dominate. Simply put, the Communists' primary concern was not with the black masses or with working people, but with the global objectives of the Soviet Union. Sooner or later these objectives were bound to conflict with the necessities of the racial struggle.

I learned this firsthand, having been for several years an active member of the Young Communist League. I was drawn to the Communists because they appeared to be the only political organization expressing any concern about racial discrimination. I first encountered Communists at a public meeting on the Scottsboro Case, where a man approached me and asked if I was interested in passing out literature in the black neighborhoods of Philadelphia. Later, after I had joined, the Communists sent me to the College of the City of New York (CCNY) where, instead of attending classes or studying, I organized for the YCL.

Eventually, I was placed in charge of a campaign to combat racial discrimination in the armed forces. This was, of course, during the period of the Hitler-Stalin pact, when World War II was referred to as Roosevelt's war of imperialism. The invasion of the USSR by Nazi Germany changed all that. Now the war was no longer an imperialistic venture, but a struggle for freedom and democracy. Everything, we were told, must be sacrificed for the war effort. This meant, of course, that my project was to be dissolved and that those blacks like A. Philip Randolph, who continued throughout the war to struggle for better racial conditions, were to be subjected to a drumfire of criticism from the Communist party. I resigned from the YCL immediately. I did so not simply because my project was being dropped, but because the Communists had now demonstrated that they were not concerned about what was happening in the United States but with what in their view was best for the Soviet Union. They were prepared to sacrifice everything, including the urgent need for improved conditions for Negroes, for the USSR.

During the early decades of the twentieth century race riots, in which blacks suffered by far the heaviest casualties, were a common occurrence. They were often triggered by the efforts of Negroes to assert their economic and social rights. The brutality which marked these outbursts—over forty Negroes were killed in a 1917 outburst in East Saint Louis, Ill.—cast a pall over the Negro community, which aspired to share in the "normalcy" and wealth which followed the conclusion of World War I.

The totality of repression, terrorism, and political indifference was to render any effort at black collective action impossible. The only alternatives were the utopian fantasies of Marcus Garvey, or some form of personal, artistic, or spiritual outlet. The prevailing sense of hopelessness contributed to the cultural phenomenon in the 1920s known as the Harlem Renaissance. Since blacks could not make revolution, either peaceably or nonpeaceably, they were forced

to write about it. Thus we have Claude McKay's famous
sonnet "If We Must Die":

> If we must die—let it not be like hogs
> Hunted and penned in an inglorious spot.
> While round us bark the mad and hungry
> dogs,
> Making their mock at our accursed lot.
> If we must die—oh, let us nobly die,
> So that our precious blood shall not be shed
> In vain; then even the monsters we defy
> Shall be constrained to honor us though
> dead!
> Oh, Kinsmen we must meet the common
> foe;
> Though far outnumbered, let us show us
> brave,
> And for their thousand blows deal one
> deathblow!
> What though before us lies the open grave?
> Like men we'll face the murderous, cow-
> ardly pack,
> Pressed to the wall, dying, but fighting
> back! [2]

If the 1920s was one of the Negro's darkest decades, the
1930s brought a new sense of hope. The Great Depression
visited itself more harshly on blacks than on anyone else.
But a series of developments set the stage for future

2. Langston Hughes and Arna Bontemps, eds., *The Poetry of the Negro,
1746–1970* (New York: Doubleday, 1970), p. 102.

progress while it relieved that feeling which Claude McKay described so appropriately as being "pressed to the wall."

The strategies of despair, symbolized by the Garvey movement, now gave way to the high expectations which accompanied the formation of the CIO. These expectations, shared by black and white alike, proved well founded. The unions which formed the nucleus of CIO strength—the autoworkers, steelworkers, mineworkers, and others—organized the mass-production industries where blacks made up an increasingly large percentage of the work force. Along with racially progressive AFL unions like the ILGWU, these CIO unions added an important dimension to the American social context, namely:

—The unions were the driving force in the fight to win substantial improvements in the material conditions of black industrial workers;

—Most of the unions were led by men who, for both practical and principled reasons, believed that black and white workers should be organized together;

—The unions hastened the end of the manipulation of black workers by employers who saw in the Negro work force a source of cheap labor, a potential strikebreaker, and a wedge which could profitably be used to depress wages;

—The unions became the first, mass interracial institution in a nation where separation had been the rule;

—And the unions presented Negroes with organizing skills and a sense of participation in an important social struggle—these would have incalculable effects on the later civil rights movement.

Like the unions, the New Deal, although it did not address the unique problems created by racial discrimination, provided indirect encouragement to the civil rights movement. The coming of the Civilian Conservation Corps, the WPA, the Wagner Act, and other programs inaugurated under FDR's administration brought an end to the laissez-faire tradition which had governed American economic affairs from the nation's birth. If the government could assist the retired with Social Security, or the jobless with unemployment benefits, why then couldn't it intervene on behalf of blacks?

The Wagner Act had a more immediate effect for blacks than other pieces of New Deal legislation because it brought to a victorious conclusion A. Philip Randolph's twelve-year campaign to organize the sleeping car porters. That victory made Randolph the best-known Negro in the United States, and it also paved the way for the emergence of the most important movement in the annals of American social struggle.

The coming of the 1940s brought a heretofore unknown coherence to the strategy of the civil rights movement. As America busied herself with wartime preparations, civil rights forces launched their assault in two directions. A. Philip Randolph and his followers organized for nonviolent, direct-action protests, and the NAACP piled case after case on the dockets of the court system.

To understand Randolph's unique ability as a civil rights leader, one must recognize that he was a product both of the Negro experience and of the radical political tradition. As a Negro, Randolph understood the depths of discrimination as no white man could; he had learned to persevere in the face of seemingly insuperable odds; and he valued racial pride and what it meant to the common black worker. From socialism Randolph had gained the ability to order and discipline his thinking; he also developed a tactical sense and, most important, he achieved an understanding of the economic underpinnings of discrimination.

It was the combination of these two traditions that gave depth to Randolph's vision and that led him to reject actively the predominant philosophical currents of the black community: Booker T. Washington's gradualism; Marcus Garvey's nationalism; and the concept that black progress would come only with the development of an educated Negro elite, the "Talented Tenth," to use the phrase of W. E. B. DuBois, its most prominent advocate.

Randolph resisted these trends and, instead, conceived and implemented the first March on Washington in 1940–41. This campaign was the symbolic inauguration of the modern civil rights movement.

The March was the first mass protest ever seriously threatened by Negro Americans, who until then had fought discrimination through court actions that were generally unsuccessful, individual acts of protest, or cultural rebellion. There had never before been an attempt at such a large-scale, collective, direct action as Randolph was then proposing.

Randolph's campaign was also the first instance of organized protest by American blacks against *economic* oppression. Earlier expressions of protest had been directed at terrorism in the South, the poll tax, the Grandfather Clause, and other of the more blatant manifestations of institutionalized Jim Crow. The organizers of the March, however, had one overriding objective: jobs for the black workers who, weary of impoverishment and shrinking opportunities in the South, were streaming into Detroit, Chicago, Los Angeles, and other urban areas of the North and West in search of a better lot in industrial America.

While these new migrants to urban life would be the ultimate beneficiaries of the March's demands, they themselves had, by the act of their migration, in fact made the March plan feasible. Until the mid 1930s and 1940s there had been no black working class large enough or concentrated enough to support a national, mass movement of the scope envisioned by Randolph.

In terms of its strategy, the March's major success was in forcing the federal government to deal with Negroes as equals for the first time in history. Black people had come a long way from those dark hours in 1917 when President Wilson had insulted Monroe Trotter, the brilliant and outspoken editor of the *Boston Guardian*, declining to take seriously Trotter's complaints concerning the rigid segregation of the District of Columbia, a segregation introduced by Wilson himself. Franklin Roosevelt had, of course, met privately with such Negro leaders as Walter White [3] and Mary McLeod Bethune, had assured them of his personal concern for the plight of southern blacks, and had then

3. Walter White was executive director of the NAACP from 1930 to 1955.

done nothing. For in truth Roosevelt would do nothing unless he was confronted with a movement that dealt from a position of strength. Whatever his inner sentiments might have been, FDR's political impulse was to ignore the complaints of blacks for fear that any positive action would divide the Democratic party and deal a mortal blow to his domestic program.

Randolph, who had only recently won his own struggle with the Pullman Company, well understood that Negroes were in no position to issue ultimatums if they were weak and unorganized. Thus, when he announced the March plans to the press, Randolph said:

> Only power can effect the enforcement and adoption of a given policy, however meritorious it may be. The virtue and rightness of a certain cause are not alone the condition and cause of its acceptance. Power and pressure are at the foundation of the march of social justice and reform. . . . Power and pressure do not reside in the few, an intelligentsia. They lie in and flow from the masses. Power does not even rest with the masses as such. Power is the active principle of only the organized masses, the masses united for a definite purpose. Hence Negro America must bring its power and pressure to bear upon the agencies and representatives of the federal government to exact their rights in National Defense Em-

ployment and the armed forces of the country. . . .[4]

Randolph also understood that racial progress would not
result from generalized complaints about the discriminatory
conditions which blacks experienced. The federal government, Randolph believed, must be presented with a concrete list of demands which, if agreed to, would bring about
measurable progress for black Americans. Furthermore,
Randolph refused to capitulate and compromise those demands even in the face of enormous pressure and even with
the promise of FDR's good intentions. Randolph demanded
the presidential guarantee, and the March was not called off
until that guarantee was set down in writing.

Executive Order 8802 was issued on June 25, 1941, a week
before the March was scheduled to take place. It banned
discrimination by defense industries and the government
and established a Fair Employment Practices Commission
to enforce the antibias decree. The executive order was not
a popular measure in the South, and the powerful southern
bloc within the Democratic party attacked the FEPC immediately. Yet despite criticism, and despite the fact that, as
the first government antibias agency the FEPC was not
overzealous in its enforcement, the first planned March on
Washington can be said to have had an enormous effect on
the economic conditions of Negroes. Prior to the executive
order, blacks had filled less than 1 percent of all defense in-
dustry jobs. Within a few years after 8802 was issued, however, blacks filled 8 percent of those jobs and had, more-

4. Anderson, *Randolph*, pp. 248, 249.

over, gained a permanent foothold in the industrial North.

The March also set crucial strategic precedents for the civil rights movement. Where there had been a vacuum, there was now a mass base of potential strength among concentrated, organized black communities. The Negro masses' tactical vision began to expand. Randolph had after all acted within a constitutional framework. He had not shut down the machinery of government or undermined the war effort. By shifting the racial struggle toward economic needs, and by blazing new trails in terms of strategy, Randolph had demonstrated that the Negro masses represented an untapped source of creative energy. For their part, Negroes were becoming increasingly aware of their potential power. There was a new sense of expectation and, in the young, impatience with the persistence of Jim Crow and the nation's apathetic response to injustice. They were determined that what had been won with the exigencies of war would not be surrendered with the war's conclusion.

Nor was Executive Order 8802 the only source of hope. At last, midway into the 1940s, the three-decades-long campaign of the NAACP in the courts was beginning to have a positive effect. Persuaded by the skillful arguments of such NAACP attorneys as Thurgood Marshall and William Hastie,[5] the Supreme Court issued a series of rulings which drove the first important wedges into the heretofore solid legal structure of Jim Crow. Laws which barred Negroes from participation in Democratic party primaries were invalidated; the Grandfather Clause was ruled unconstitutional; the right of blacks to enter into collective bargaining

5. In 1949 William Hastie was appointed the first Negro federal judge in United States history.

agreements was upheld. And, in the most momentous decision to that date, the Supreme Court ruled, in 1946, that
segregated seating in interstate transportation was unconstitutional.

With the *Irene Morgan* decision, as the ruling on interstate
transportation was known,[6] and the success of A. Philip
Randolph's March on Washington, the civil rights movement was confronted with a dramatically different situation.
The combination of direct action and legal action was forcing the nation to confront the call for racial equality. Both
the federal government and the courts had, with much
prodding, begun to admit not merely the existence of discrimination, but also their own obligation under the Con-
stitution to correct its more apparent manifestations. Blacks
and their white allies were in turn encouraged to seek out
new targets, and to experiment with different, more daring
tactics of direct action.

Thus it was only natural that an organization committed
to the spread of such nonviolent techniques of direct action
should form around the goals of the Negro movement. The
Congress of Racial Equality was just such an organization.

The CORE that was founded in 1942 bears little resem-
blance to the CORE of today. The early CORE was established by individuals passionately dedicated to the prin-

6. *Irene Morgan* decision: *Morgan* v. *Commonwealth of Virginia*. Irene
Morgan refused to move to the rear of a Greyhound bus that was traveling
from Virginia to Washington, D.C., and was subsequently convicted in the
lower Virginia courts for violating a state statute requiring segregation of
the races on all public vehicles. The United States Supreme Court ultimately ruled that the Virginia law could not apply to interstate passengers.
The ruling was of such a nature that it lent itself to application on railroads,
in airplanes, etc.

ciple of integration; today's CORE is run by black
segregationists. Roy Innis, its current national director,
preaches a crude brand of separatism.[7] He advocated Senate
confirmation of G. Harrold Carswell to the Supreme Court
on the ground that Carswell's apparent hostility to integration would help balance the Court's integrationist majority.
Even more celebrated was Innis's conference with Lester
Maddox and other Dixiecrats who met in an effort to devise
a formula to reinstitute dual school systems.

The philosophical framework which guided CORE in its
early years was rooted in a far different tradition from those
underlying black nationalism and black capitalism. It was
founded by pacifists, mostly members of the Fellowship of
Reconciliation.[8] Democracy, integration, and nonviolence
were its hallmark principles, and its activists were scrupu-
lous in their adherence to these doctrines. Officers were
democratically elected, and all protest campaigns were carefully discussed before they were implemented. Up to 1966
all of CORE's protest campaigns were models of biracial co-
operation, and all of its campaigns were carried out peacefully, without disruption or violence on the part of the demonstrators.

CORE's principles were Mohandas Gandhi's principles.
Next to A. Philip Randolph, Gandhi had more direct influence on the development of a civil rights strategy during the
1940s than any other individual, here or abroad. Gandhi

7. Roy Innis, a black nationalist and exponent of "neo-Garveyism," was
elected national director of CORE in 1968.
8. The Fellowship of Reconciliation is a religious-pacifist organization, a
number of whose activists made important contributions to the civil rights
movement.

Marcus Garvey, founder of the Universal Negro Improvement Association, advocated black unity, chauvinism, and the return to Africa. In 1921 he announced the creation of the Empire of Africa and named himself president. He was convicted of mail fraud in 1923, imprisoned, and deported in 1927.

*Wide World Photos*

*United Press International*

A leader of the Negro civil rights movement for over fifty years, A. Philip Randolph founded the Brotherhood of Sleeping Car Porters, the first Negro trade union to receive an international charter from the American Federation of Labor. He was president of the union from 1925 to 1968, and in 1957 was elected the first Negro vice-president of the AFL-CIO.

Randolph, Mrs. Eleanor Roosevelt, and Fiorello H. LaGuardia, the mayor of New York City, meet in 1946 at a rally at Madison Square Garden to save the Fair Employment Practices Commission.
*United Press International*

Mrs. Rosa Parks, right, being fingerprinted by a deputy sheriff in Montgomery, Ala. in February 1956. Mrs. Parks's refusal to give her bus seat to a white passenger sparked the Montgomery bus boycott.

*Wide World Photos*

At left, Dr. Martin Luther King, Jr., accompanied by Dr. Ralph Abernathy, being booked by a Montgomery police lieutenant on Feb. 23, 1956. The leader of the Montgomery bus boycott, King was arrested on several indictments arising out of the boycott.

*Wide World Photos*

Below, King, A. Philip Randolph, and Roy Wilkins announce plans for a prayer pilgrimage to Washington on May 17, 1957, the third anniversary of the Supreme Court's decision to abolish segregation in American public schools.
*Wide World Photos*

Above, federal troops escort black students away from Central High School in Little Rock, Ark. In September 1957 Orval Faubus, the governor of Arkansas, called out the national guard to prevent integration of Central High School. Riots broke out, and President Eisenhower sent federal troops to maintain order. He also placed the national guard under federal control to insure that integration of the school would be achieved.

*Wide World Photos*

Left, Negro demonstrators stage a sit-in at a segregated lunch counter in Little Rock, Ark.

*Wide World Photos*

Below, firemen in Birmingham, Ala. turn a firehose on Negro demonstrators.

*Wide World Photos*

Undaunted by the jeers of white hecklers, a group of black demonstrators in Bogalusa, Ala. march to the city hall to present a petition requesting equal police protection. *Wide World Photos*

Below, Police Commissioner Bull Connor directs the arrests of a group of black demonstrators in Birmingham, Ala. on April 10, 1963. *Wide World Photos*

Left, unoccupied seats of the Mississippi delegation at the 1964 Democratic National Convention at Atlantic City, N.J. The credentials of the all-white Mississippi delegation were challenged by a black delegation composed of Mississippi Freedom Democrats. Both groups rejected a compromise offered by officials of the Democratic party.

Below, a 1965 civil rights protest march in Montgomery, Ala. is led by Dr. Martin Luther King, Jr. To his left is Dr. Ralph Bunche.

*Wide World Photos*

Right, a quiet Sunday in Watts, Calif. in August 1965. Only a few days earlier the area had been devastated by riots in which angry Negroes vented their frustration by burning and looting. At the riots' end, 34 people were dead, 1,032 were injured, and property damage was estimated at about 40 million dollars.

*Wide World Photos*

Right, a national guardsman patrols a Detroit intersection during the riot of July 1967. Considered the worst racial riot in American history, the Detroit violence lasted four days and left 14 square miles of the city destroyed by fire, 41 people dead, and damage estimated at 250 million dollars.

*Wide World Photos*

Dr. Martin Luther King, Jr., delivers his famous "I Have A Dream" speech during the 1963 March on Washington.

believed that social movements must evolve democratically, and that those who participate in a specific movement must give their services willingly, without economic or physical coercion. To be completely democratic and genuinely progressive, he believed, a movement must have the support and participation of all oppressed races and classes. He thus insisted that the lowest class in India, the untouchables, become a part of his political party. He taught that no movement can survive simply by having the correct program, or by following intelligent tactics. A movement must also possess a relationship to, and have an understanding of, the roots of the social struggle in which it is engaged. Without such an understanding, Gandhi felt, a social movement will ultimately collapse from a lack of discipline.

To understand Gandhi, one must keep in mind that his philosophy is always related to the specific conditions in India. But his wisdom often has a universal application. Certainly the history of the civil rights movement bears out his assertions about the need for understanding the historical background of the black man's struggle.

Why, then, in the mid-1960s did factions within the black community turn their backs on Gandhi and adopt instead the rhetoric of revolution, when in fact armed struggle was both implausible and irrelevant? Why did the New Left embrace violence, knowing full well that interracial violence has historically visited itself most terribly on the black masses?

Part of the answer is that the advocates of Black Power in fact lacked precisely what they chided other, less vocally militant leaders for failing to acquire. They lacked a sense of black history, of black culture, and of the tradition and ethos of American Negroes. These militants spoke of "culture" and "history," but the culture and history they described were artificial and self-imposed. Their roots were not planted in the firm ground of personal experience, but in the hardened soil of despair and in the substanceless soil of fantasy.

For most Negro Americans, a sense of their heritage arises naturally out of personal experience. Even my own early background, though it was in many ways atypical, was sufficient for such a feeling to implant itself.

I was born in West Chester, Pa., a town rich in the history and culture of Negro Americans. There was a strong Quaker tradition in West Chester, and it became an important stop on the Underground Railroad in the period leading up to the Civil War. The antislavery sentiment of the inhabitants was revealed in the town's architecture, for beneath its aging, Colonial homes ran hidden passageways which had concealed runaway slaves from the southern plantation owners who had journeyed north to reclaim their "property," and from bounty hunters—men who collected fees for each runaway captured and returned to his southern master. A few miles away was the town of Christiana, where Negroes collectively and violently repulsed a Maryland slaveholder searching for a runaway in what was to become one of the most celebrated incidents of the abolitionist era, the Christiana Riot.

Thus, while West Chester was certainly no utopia of interracial harmony—indeed, "segregation" and "discrimination" were two of the first words that had significant meaning for me—the extent of racism was not so deep as to prevent a black youngster from becoming aware of his cultural and historical heritage. In this I was more fortunate than most blacks. West Chester was not the deep South, with its rigid, enforced Jim Crow and its shambles of an educational system. Nor was it the archetypal northern ghetto, with its malignant pattern of social dislocation. The high school I attended was integrated, and while—because of my blackness—I was deprived of honors I had earned, my intellectual and athletic achievements were recognized. Moreover, West Chester's black community was economically and socially heterogeneous. It included occasional representatives of the "black bourgeoisie," mainly businessmen and property owners; working-class blacks, some of whom were struggling to break the bonds of impoverishment; and others who had given up the struggle—the down-and-outers.

From these diverse people and their diverse experiences, I learned about my own heritage. They sang me Negro ballads, quoted me Negro poetry, and recited folktales told by slaves. I met black ministers, black political leaders, and black visionaries. And through all these encounters, I gained an understanding of the Negro struggle. This happened simply because these indigenous forms are about precisely that. They tell of the struggles of blacks, first against slavery and then against discrimination. They are, in short, chronicles of my history.

So the raw materials are present for the Negro rebel. He is already in touch with his past, if he only troubles to look for it. He can easily attain a sense of the history of the Negro struggle.

However, Gandhi did not teach that the rebel's point of view should be purely subjective, as some contemporary militants would have it. Gandhi insisted that the struggle include and appeal not only to the rebels themselves but also to a majority of the community. As Gandhi taught, a social movement relying on the tactics of nonviolence cannot succeed unless it is able to convince a full majority of the people that its cause is just. Thus, when CORE members defied southern tradition in the 1940s and 1950s and refused to submit to segregation, they were fortified with the knowledge that *most* Americans approved their acts. By the same token, the confrontationist tactics of New Left-inspired students during the 1960s failed in the long run to win any permanent or far-reaching changes. Instead they provoked a widespread counterreaction for the very reason that most Americans did not sympathize with their tactics, their values, or their programs.

Gandhi also taught that, in a situation where the objectives of a social movement are accepted as valid by the majority, protest becomes an effective tactic to the degree that it elicits brutality and oppression from the power structure. One can readily understand the full implications of this theory. It was not the civil rights movement's program which aroused the conscience of the nation, but the sight of small children entering a Little Rock high school accompanied by a federal troop escort that could not protect them from the jeering cadences of an ugly and irrational mob. Negroes gained moral authority not because Americans opposed segregation, but because black people were suffering, because churches were bombed and children firehosed.

The conclusion of World War II brought an altered domestic situation which encouraged CORE to test out the Gandhian principles that had provided the organization's philosophical undergirding. The time was propitious, we believed, because it was apparent to all that the nation's attitudes on the race question were undergoing a slow but profound change. Negroes were growing increasingly intolerant of injustice. This was particularly true of returning troops who expected something tangible in return for their contribution to the war effort. The immediate postwar period was a time of prosperity, and many Americans felt that blacks should share in this wealth. The public was beginning to be persuaded that Jim Crow was morally wrong, and the South was learning that its traditions were not shared by the nation.

National sentiment was changing. The Supreme Court was becoming more sympathetic, and the federal government, after much prodding, was becoming more responsive. The institutions of American society were treating the racial question from a point of view totally different from that they had espoused fifteen years earlier.

In light of these developments, CORE was stimulated to undertake a protest campaign that would provide a direct challenge to Jim Crow. Our campaign was called the Journey of Reconciliation, and it consisted of interracial groups riding the buses and trains of the upper South to test the *Irene Morgan* decision. Blacks sat in the sections of the bus reserved for whites, while the white demonstrators sat in the back, in the "colored" section. We limited the campaign to the states of the upper South, believing that to extend the protests into Mississippi, Alabama, or other deep South states would invite certain violence.

Our purpose in launching the Journey of Reconciliation was educational. We felt it necessary to explode the myth, widely circulated by the South, that black people were content with and in fact favored segregation. My feeling about this process of education was deep and personal. I can recall one occasion when having gotten on a bus and passed by a white child seated near the front with his mother, I realized, after I had found a seat in the back, the injustice I had committed. By my very act of submitting to segregation, by my submission to discrimination, I had reinforced in that child's mind the stereotype of the southern Negro as happy in his state of servility. I had damaged the Negro people's struggle for freedom as well, by making it that much more difficult to convince whites that we hated the role society assigned to us. It was then that I vowed never to sit in the back of the bus again.

Some blacks regarded the participants in the Journey of Reconciliation with scarcely muted hostility. Those with a vested stake in the status quo, who profited financially or psychologically from the Negro's place of inferiority in the social order, were not enthusiastic about the restiveness of black youth or pacifist demonstrators. They were often professional people, like the black schoolteacher in Chapel Hill, N.C., who actually got down on his knees and beseeched me to stop making trouble and move to the back of the bus.

This man did not represent the majority of southern Negroes. The masses were not yet ready to enter into active struggle, but their sympathies were with us. They waited and watched, hoping for the emergence of a strategy that would lead to the creation of a mass movement in which they could participate with a realizable expectation of broad change.

The renewed activities of A. Philip Randolph were also

drawing the attention of black people. Randolph's second mass-action effort, launched in 1947, was directed at one of the most rigidly segregated major institutions of American society—the armed services. Randolph demanded an executive order, similar to the earlier one issued by Roosevelt, that would abolish Jim Crow in the military. And he promised that, should President Truman fail to respond, a call would go out to all young black men to refuse conscription into the army. This was indeed a bold gesture, made more audacious because many in the nation believed Randolph might actually follow through on his threat; he had pledged "to oppose a Jim Crow army till I rot in jail." [9]

While Randolph was prepared to take considerable risks, to perform illegal acts of civil disobedience, and to push protest tactics to their limit, he was not prepared to cross the line from nonviolent protest into violent action. Always, he retained his basic faith in nonviolence. He saw nonviolence in absolute terms; there could be no compromise, no capitulation to the despair which breeds violence. As Randolph explained to a Senate committee:

> We would participate in no overt
> acts against our government . . .
> ours would be one of non-resistance . . .
> ours would be one of non-cooperation;
> ours would be one of non-participation
> in the military forces of the country. . . .
> We would be willing to absorb the,
> violence, absorb the terrorism, to
> face the music and to take whatever

9. Anderson, *Randolph*, p. 278.

> comes, and we, as a matter of fact
> consider that we are more loyal to
> our country than the people who
> perpetrate segregation and discrimination
> on Negroes because of color or race.[10]

And while there were those among the established black leadership who expressed reservations about a campaign of civil disobedience directed at the draft, the sentiments of the young, including returning veterans, was overwhelmingly favorable. Executive Order 9981, calling for an end to military discrimination "as rapidly as possible," was signed by President Truman on July 26, 1948. The decree was a testimony to Randolph's careful daring, his sense of timing and strategy.

But it symbolized much more than that. It reflected the changing temper of the country and of its political institutions. At the same time that Randolph was discussing the possibility of resisting the draft, the Democratic party was in the midst of adopting the strongest race-relations platform in the history of any of the major political parties.

In an open rebuff to the Dixiecrats, the party's liberal wing, led by Hubert Humphrey, pushed through a platform that addressed itself to the specific economic and social injustices suffered by racial minorities. It called for an anti-lynching bill, a voting rights measure, the establishment of a permanent FEPC, integration in interstate travel, home rule for Washington, D.C., and the creation of a civil rights commission and a civil rights division within the Justice Department.

10. Anderson, *Randolph*, p. 278.

This platform represented a sharp break from the political programs of the past, which spoke in generalized language about the sanctity of democratic freedoms, while offering no concrete proposals for relieving the misery of the oppressed. But perhaps equally as important, the platform signified an acknowledgement of the growing importance of the Negro vote, which was in fact to play a crucial role in the close, four-party presidential contest that year.

Thus another mass institution, this time the political party which the South had considered its own, bowed to the considerable weight of the Negro protest movement. In 1919 the NAACP had issued its program for human dignity; thirty years later the political process, so long closed to black people, was recognizing these demands as valid.

The 1950s are usually characterized as a decade of apathy, highlighted by McCarthyism, the mediocrity of the Eisenhower administration, and a narrowing of America's social vision. Certainly the 1950's was an unlikely time for the birth of successful protest movements or revolutionary challenges to mass institutions.

And in fact it seemed, at the decade's outset, that despite its urgency, the civil rights agenda would have to await a more propitious time, when the hysteria of the right had abated and the left had overcome its fatigue. The expectations raised in 1948 by Harry Truman's forthright racial programs were to be dashed on the rocks of congressional indifference and the intransigence of the still-powerful southern bloc. Thus, while Truman had proposed an extensive package of antidiscrimination measures, not one bill passed Congress.

A vacuum was left by the decline of radical political movements that had once been ideologically influential. The radical parties had never fared well at electoral politics; their role had been that of theoretical vanguard. They had been tireless in pointing out the injustices of the capitalist system and in calling for legislation that would curb specific abuses. Social Security, labor legislation, unemployment compensation— demands for these had formed the substance of the Socialist program years before

2
the
protest
era

they were transformed into law. But now the radical parties were impotent, having succumbed to the persecutions of Joseph McCarthy and their own mistaken assumptions about American society.

Within the Democratic party, the liberals who were instrumental in formulating and pushing through the civil rights plank at the 1948 party convention were unable to sustain the impetus generated by that struggle. Their program was beaten back in Congress, while the party's mantle of leadership passed to individuals possessing a discernible lack of feeling for race issues. To Adlai Stevenson, the struggle against racial discrimination was more a potential liability than an opportunity for moving the party forward. He did not seek to enlist blacks in his crusade for the presidency in 1952. In a southward gesture that was a clear signal of retreat, Stevenson selected Alabama's John Sparkman as his running mate. The Democratic party's 1952 platform was without substance, proposing little of positive merit to curb the widespread abuses of Jim Crow.

The Republican party's attitude was even worse. As a military leader, General Eisenhower had shown himself no friend of the Negro, having on several different occasions made special trips to Washington to testify against the abolition of Jim Crow in the armed forces. His political philosophy was a warmed-over version of traditional Republican laissez-faire. The federal government's role in social and economic affairs should be reduced, he said, staking out a position hardly designed to arouse the enthusiasm of those whose first glimmerings of hope were the result of government intervention in domestic policy.

These uninspiring political developments came in the

wake of disturbing economic trends. The boom of the post-war years had subsided; unemployment was on the rise. And as has historically been the case, blacks felt the most immediate and widespread impact of the deterioriating economic picture. Unemployment among black workers rose from 5.9 percent in 1948, to 9.9 percent in 1954, to over 12 percent in 1958. And the gap between the black and white median income, which had been steadily narrowing since the conclusion of World War II, began to widen once again, so that where the average black family had earned 57 percent of what its white counterpart was earning in 1951, by 1958 the median black income was but 51 percent of median white income.

In sum, political and economic institutions were re-trenching. The consensus which seemed within our grasp had eluded us. America was lapsing into passivity.

Among the major institutions of government, only the courts did not reflect the weakening of national will. Adhering to a pattern established in the late 1930s and the 1940s, the Supreme Court continued to hand down decisions which hastened the desegregation process. In 1948 the high court ordered the state of Oklahoma to provide law school facilities to Negroes. Two years later it directed Oklahoma to end the segregation of its university graduate school, and it ordered the University of Texas to integrate its law school.

These directives were but a prelude to the 1954 order, the now-famous *Brown* decision, which ruled that segregated school systems violated the equal protection guarantee of the Fourteenth Amendment. There is no need to discuss here the legal implications of that case. However, I think it is important to understand a few of the *Brown* decision's political and social consequences.

—First, *Brown* defined the arenas of struggle for the coming period. When blacks marched, demonstrated, and litigated, the target was now to be the schools. And similarly, when the South plotted its strategy of "massive resistance," its principal objective was to forestall school desegregation.

—Second, because *Brown* affected in a fundamental way one of the most important socializing institutions of society, it touched the lives of millions of whites in a direct and personal way. Therefore Americans were now forced to confront the meaning and future implications of Negro demands.

—Third, *Brown* signified that at least one arm of government, the judiciary, was the unambiguous ally of the black man. The knowledge that they could count on the courts for redress fortified southern blacks with a new sense of confidence. If the Supreme Court had *upheld* dual school systems, it is unlikely Rosa Parks would have refused to move to the back of the bus; [1] there would have been no Montgomery bus boycott; no Dr. King, and the whole course

1. On December 1, 1955 Mrs. Rosa Parks was arrested for refusing to move to the back of a Montgomery bus. Her arrest angered the black community and ignited the bus boycott.

of the civil rights movement would have been set years back.

—Fourth, the *Brown* decision represented a head-on challenge to the legal fabric of segregation and thus evoked immediate and widespread reaction from the South's political leadership. In its most extreme manifestation, the resistance devised by the South amounted to a unique form of civil disobedience, in which entire governmental units defied federal law and watched passively while white citizens brutalized black citizens. The result was not the inhibition of integration, as the South had hoped, but the isolation of the South itself from the rest of the nation and ultimately the hastening of the breakdown of its system of racial stratification.

As the *Brown* decision also broadened the arena of protest, it imposed on the various civil rights groups a sense of unity which was a necessary precondition for more substantial progress. The NAACP, with its middle-class constituency, favored a legalistic approach; CORE, comprised of pacifist radicals, engaged in highly disciplined but individualized direct action; and A. Philip Randolph, drawing from his socialist and labor traditions, pioneered in mass-action campaigns.

Each group had been working towards a common object. And each had cooperated with the others, e.g., when CORE members were arrested, the NAACP often provided legal aid. The NAACP and CORE also held joint discussions to determine when and where protests might take place and what tactics might be appropriate.

Each group had, however, a tactic it tended to prefer, often because it suited the style of the organization's social base. But with new opportunities opening up, these groups now found it imperative to move closer together. Where once they had been satisfied to work separately, now they could *not* afford not to work together.

Parenthetically, I would like to point out that the NAACP was not merely legalistically oriented. For decades it was the bedrock of the Negro movement, particularly in isolated areas of the rural South too forbidding for northern activists. Following the *Brown* decision, the Mississippi White Citizens' Council, which described the NAACP as a "left-wing, power mad organ of destruction," carried out a systematic campaign of terrorism and economic coercion in an unsuccessful effort to crush the organization.[2] The WCC compiled lists of NAACP members. Negroes who were members, or who were suspected of being members, were either fired from their jobs, or if they owned a business, were refused credit by white banks and white suppliers. In addition to financial reprisal, those known to hold leadership positions in the NAACP suffered beatings and saw their homes burned. A few, particularly those conducting voter-registration drives, were murdered, sometimes in plain day, with never so much as a single arrest made.

2. The White Citizens' Council, comprised largely of businessmen, has been described as the "Ku Klux Klan in business suits." It spearheaded white resistance to desegregation through economic reprisals by attempting to buy off black leaders and, ultimately, through violence.

The growing unity within the civil rights movement was not so much a matter of conscious choice as the result of objective necessity. Strategy had to be refined if the victories won in the courtroom were to be enforced in states that were preaching open defiance of the law. Symbolic success was no longer enough. The *Brown* decision meant nothing *unless Southern schools were desegregated.* A hit-or-miss pattern of protest could never bring about massive changes in the South. Nor could a movement limited to a small ideological cadre. Now entire black communities had to be mobilized.

The 1955 Montgomery bus boycott was the first successful mass-protest campaign in the South. Today Montgomery is well remembered for having thrust Martin Luther King into a position of national leadership. But at that time Montgomery meant even more. The strong sense of unity and purpose exhibited by the Negro community, the ability of the black citizens to sustain the boycott through month after weary month, their renewed determination in the face of violence all served as an example to the blacks across the South who were thirsting for a movement that could actually threaten basic southern institutions. The Montgomery boycott was important for other reasons also. It was one of the first protests in which the demands of the black community were comprehensive enough to include both economic rights and human dignity. The Montgomery demands included the abolition of segregated seating patterns, an end to the abusive behavior of white bus drivers, and the hiring of blacks as drivers.

Although there had been previous boycott campaigns, usually "Buy Black" efforts in northern ghettoes, Montgomery marked the first successful use of the boycott in the South. The concessions won in the earlier campaigns had been of a short-term nature, generally limited to a few black businesses. They had very little effect on the larger pattern of employment discrimination. The Montgomery boycott changed all that because it was the first time an entire black community acted together.

The triumphant conclusion of the boycott presented King with a unique problem. Although he had won a victory hitherto undreamed of, there was nothing to guarantee that this one isolated triumph would lead to broader gains. For Dr. King, the question was how to sustain the spirit of Montgomery.

As an aide to Dr. King, I felt that without a victory at Montgomery, the southern protest movement, then showing its first signs of life, would die stillborn. I also felt that a victory at Montgomery would have no permanent meaning in the racial struggle unless it led to the achievement of dozens of similar victories throughout the South.

In practical terms, this meant that the movement needed a sustaining mechanism that could translate what we had learned during the bus boycott into a broad strategy for protest in the South. At the same time we felt it vital that we maintain the psychological momentum Montgomery had generated. If nothing else, we needed at least to appear to be moving ahead, attacking new targets, testing new tactics, and pressing the movement forward.

The sustaining mechanism that finally evolved was the Southern Christian Leadership Conference. Today the SCLC is in eclipse, saddled with financial and organizational burdens which I fear are too formidable to overcome.

But for over a decade, during the height of the era of protest, the SCLC was the dynamic center of the civil rights
movement. And in the story of its rise and decline lie important clues to the successes and shortcomings of the entire civil rights protest movement.

To understand the nature of the SCLC requires a familiar-
ity with the unique structure of the southern Negro church.
The structure of the SCLC was patterned after that of the
church, and its style rooted in the church's traditions.

This close identification with the Negro church proved a
source of strength at the outset. Ultimately, however, it contained the seeds of the SCLC's destruction.

There were sound reasons for the church becoming the
SCLC's organizational base. The church was one of the few
institutions which communicated with the broad mass of
working people. Moreover, it was the only institution indigenous to the black community. Black churches did not
need to depend on white money for survival. Short of outright terror tactics, southern whites had nothing to use as a
lever on the church.

Like the black church, the structure of the SCLC was au-
tocratic. In the church, the pastor's autonomy was almost
total. In the SCLC, major decisions rested with Dr. King.
He determined when and where an action would take place,
what tactics would be employed, when a campaign should
be accelerated, and when compromises should be made.
Years later, the lack of a democratic framework was to contribute to SCLC's decline. But in its early years a highly
centralized structure was essential because the movement
so often operated under crisis conditions. Members of the
SCLC were regularly beaten; many were jailed on almost

any pretext; and they faced an unending stream of law suits. Decisions had to be made as quickly and efficiently as possible and by someone who was fully informed on all aspects of the movement.

The high moral tone of the Baptist preacher well suited the movement since most of the issues than being raised were moral issues. When civil rights leaders cried out, as clergymen had before them, "Treat Us Like Men," the black masses responded.

Moreover, the movement needed an emotional dimension to whip up the enthusiasm of people who might soon be faced with economic hardship or physical danger. And no one could bring a crowd to an emotional pitch like the black preacher.

Indeed, the virtues praised by the black preacher ultimately became the strengths of the civil rights movement. Perseverance and courage—characteristics extolled from the pulpit each Sunday—became more important than intellectual or political analysis. It took enormous bravery for ordinary citizens to continue their march through streets riddled with the hate-filled eyes of white southerners, not to mention the clubs, the firehoses, and the dogs. It took an incredible level of self-control and considerable faith in one's leadership to refrain from retaliating when beaten or spat upon.

Thus when judging the SCLC, one must place above all else its most magnificent accomplishment: the creation of a disciplined mass movement of southern blacks; black people, moreover, who were not hard-core political activists, but ordinary people—church women, workers, and students. There had been nothing in the annals of American social struggle to equal this phenomenon, and there probably never will be again.

Having once built an organization whose imprint on American society can never be erased, why is the SCLC now in danger of becoming a historical relic? The answer is simply this: the civil rights struggle underwent a period of profound transition in the mid-1960s, and the SCLC failed to recognize that important changes were taking place.

The most obvious reflection of the SCLC's inability to adapt to the new needs of the transition period was its continued reliance on the tactics of protest after the potential usefulness of those tactics had been exhausted. Some observers believe that the SCLC encountered difficulties because the nation had begun to weary of demonstrations. This may be true, but the nation's mood is not what dissipated the impact of protest. Once the civil rights movement had achieved substantial victories—had in fact secured its basic social agenda—those very victories created the need for the development of a new strategic approach. After adoption of the Civil Rights Act of 1964 and the Voting Rights Act of 1965, the agenda spelled out at the March on Washington in 1963 had been secured in all but one important respect. Our economic demands—the need for more and better jobs, an expanded housing program, better education as well as integrated schools—had still to be won. Economic demands are not won by the same means as legislative demands. When one goes about trying to produce a basic transformation of the economic structure, one does not proceed by picketing or planning sit-ins. Economic reform is a political problem and the only means of achieving this reform, short of resorting to totalitarian means, is through political organization.

One point about the nature of protest should be added here. Ideally, when an individual is protesting society's refusal to acknowledge his dignity as a human being, his very act of protest has an inherent ennobling quality that confers dignity on him. But when the protester not only fails to achieve his objective, but is also unable to evoke the respect and sympathy of his fellowman, he risks a distortion of the protest process. For protest to succeed, it must produce a feeling of moving ahead; it must force people to take notice of injustice; and it must win new allies. But when it is unable to generate that momentum, protest turns inward, breeding despair and impotence. This sense of protest gone sour is one of the factors that led to the decline of the civil rights movement in the 1960s. When protest would not bring about the desired ends, tactics were escalated. Confrontation replaced strict nonviolence, and there were even occasional flareups. Protest became not simply irrelevant, but counterproductive.

Moving from protest to politics required a shift within the structure of the civil rights organization. We began to need more democracy. While it is feasible for a small group of leaders to determine the specifics of a protest demonstration without evoking dissension within the rank and file, that same small group cannot impose political decisions on the membership. Political decisions cannot be issued from above. They must be made after thorough discussion in which all who are interested have an opportunity to participate. To reach political decisions by other than democratic means is to invite division and disaster.

The problems just discussed emerged later in the SCLC's career. As was noted, the SCLC was well suited, both organizationally and temperamentally, to assume the mantle of civil rights leadership in the mid-1950s.

The SCLC's effectiveness during this period was in large part due to its strict adherence to nonviolence, which contrasted sharply with the ugly and vicious eruptions of the southern response. The violence of the South became, in fact, an organizing dynamic that stimulated many Americans out of their ambivalence about specific Negro demands for civil rights on the one hand, and about the case for the South on the other. It forced Americans, North and South, to take a stand.

It was ironic that southern brutality, which had been employed for a century to subdue the potential spirit of Negro protest, now worked to the Negro's advantage. Lynchings had not been uncommon during previous decades. What generally happened, though, was that after incidences of violence Negroes simply vanished into the backwoods and swamps of the Mississippi Delta, never to be seen or heard from again. Perhaps even more frightening than the fact of the violence was the tacit sanction given it by southern officials, who either averted their eyes or actively participated in it.

Why, was the situation different? Why was lynching an effective means of keeping the black community in check in 1925, when thirty years later such violence only seemed to make blacks more determined?

There are two basic reasons, I believe, for this shift. First, there was a qualitative difference between the kind of violence practiced in the 1920s and 1930s and that employed during the 1950s and 1960s. Dragging an anonymous Negro from jail and lynching him is a shocking and outrageous act, but it can be protested only as an isolated incident. The bombing of Dr. King's home, which happened during the Montgomery campaign, added a political dimension to southern white brutality. It was no longer just mob violence; it had become political terrorism. To a nation with roots in democratic traditions, political terrorism is the irredeemable first link in a chain leading ultimately to the total destruction of society. Political terrorism could not be ignored, let alone condoned, as the mob violence had been. Americans in their own interest had no choice but to rise up against it.

The second, and probably the more important reason southern violence backfired in the 1950s was the growing influence of television. With the coming of television, the violence of the South was no longer tucked away from the nation's attention. Now all eyes were focused on Little Rock, New Orleans, and Birmingham, transfixed by the sight of howling mobs and bombed-out churches. Were it not for the presence of those television cameras, people would never have seen the agony of children braving the screaming mob in Little Rock. Nor would Martin Luther King have emerged a national spokesman for black Americans.

Moreover, this new instantaneous and extensive coverage of the civil rights protest destroyed whatever small claim the South had had to moral or legal legitimacy. As the TV viewer saw it, the South was not holding a dialogue with black people; it was attempting to crush them by any means at hand. For the many Americans who had been ambivalent about Negro demands, television coverage was the determining factor in solidifying their views. As the cameras laid bare the southern lies, public opinion turned against the South. As the public witnessed the South's violent response to the law of the land there seemed no choice but support for those who were the victims of that violence.

Later on, however, the influence of television was to become less positive. At first the media had concentrated its attention on the civil rights movement, but little by little some black leaders began to seek out the media, to play at militancy for the benefit of the television audience. Television encouraged the rise of "instant" leaders, individuals who left no lasting imprint, but who nevertheless contributed to the image of the black man as antiwhite, violence prone, and emburdened with hate.

In its early days, though, television was clearly a boon to the civil rights struggle. Businessmen and chambers of commerce across the South dreaded the cameras. They feared bad press because they did not want another Little Rock. It would be bad for business. Therefore the business community across the South found itself able to reach a settlement with civil rights forces. Restaurants were integrated, and some blacks were hired in department stores. In some cases schools were desegregated, and municipal bus systems ended their patterns of segregated seating—generally because the chamber of commerce rather than the government decided to acquiesce to black demands. In this respect, the business community was more farsighted than the southern

political leader, who manipulated the racial issue dem-
agogically in the battle for votes. Businessmen, of course,
were not running for election. They were concerned with
profits, and they understood that the profit-making odds
were better in trying to integrate peacefully rather than in
running the risk of bad publicity or an economic boycott by
the black community.

By 1960, the nation could clearly see the fruits of the civil
rights movement. Social and political institutions had in
small measure been made to bend. We had captured the attention of the news media and won sympathy from the general public. Legal action continued to produce important
breakthroughs. Black people were themselves becoming increasingly more conscious of the civil rights struggle.

Then, the nation's political leadership finally took notice.
In 1960, both Republicans and Democrats, for the first time,
endorsed the *Brown* decision and adopted strong civil rights
positions during their national conventions. For both parties this represented a distinct break from past practice. The
influence of the South had generally been sufficient to keep
the Democratic party's liberal wing in check on civil rights
issues. As for the Republicans, their president and symbolic
standard-bearer had made relatively little contribution to
the advancement of racial equality, considering the opportunities before him. Ironically, however, Eisenhower left office an unpopular figure throughout much of the South because he was perceived as having been a champion of civil
rights. In truth, Eisenhower did the minimum expected of
the chief of state. Privately, he opposed the *Brown* decision,
endorsing it only to the extent he was forced as president to
uphold the law of the land. He made no effort to begin the

process of *enforcing* school desegregation, leaving that task to the courts, and he opposed the shutting off of federal aid to school districts that had not complied. As for his sending in troops to Little Rock, this was not, as the South believed, an unprecedented display of federal power, but a very late response to a governor who was defying the federal courts.

By the end of his second term, it had become apparent to both parties that Eisenhower's moderate approach was inadequate. In the subsequent presidential campaign, Nixon and Kennedy tried to outdo each other, each promising a more vigorous civil rights policy than his opponent.

On October 26, 1960, in the waning weeks of the campaign, John Kennedy did something of enormous symbolic importance. He made a long-distance call to Coretta King, conveying to her his sympathy and support for her husband, who was at that time behind prison bars. (King had been sentenced to four months at hard labor for leading a sit-in at an Atlanta, Ga. restaurant.) The same day that John Kennedy called Mrs. King, his brother Robert called the judge who had passed sentence on Dr. King to ask that he be released. And on the following day King was set free.

In telephoning Mrs. King, John Kennedy was paying tribute to the power of the Negro vote. But he was also taking a substantial risk of further alienating the South, where his Catholicism was already expected to be a factor against him. As events transpired that telephone call may have decided the election, for Kennedy improved significantly on the black vote accorded Stevenson in 1956 and won the support of many southern blacks—Dr. King's father for one—who usually supported the party of Lincoln.

Comparing Kennedy's attitudes with the attitudes of previous Democratic presidents shows clearly how far blacks had advanced. Under Woodrow Wilson, segregation was extended and the pleas of Negro leaders went unanswered. Under Franklin Roosevelt, blacks won some concessions, but only after threats of mass marches and civil disobedience. Harry Truman improved on Roosevelt's record, but here again, Truman simply reacted to the relentless prodding of Negro leaders like A. Philip Randolph.

Kennedy's telephone call clearly demonstrated that the Negro's position in American politics had changed. Where black leaders had had to beg and cajole and threaten to win the most minimal gains, now political leaders were coming into the black community with offerings. They promised to help in the Negro's struggle, and they acknowledged the legitimacy and importance of the Negro leaders. This was an important step toward achieving the consensus of national support we had long sought.

With the 1963 March on Washington, the civil rights movement did achieve this consensus. A few months prior to the March, only a small percentage of Americans considered civil rights the nation's most pressing problem. But following the March, that small percentage had turned into a decisive majority. The March was clearly responsible for this change in attitude.

In assessing the March's importance, one must keep in mind that America has historically been unfavorably disposed to public displays of protest. Americans may sympathize with the conditions of the oppressed, but marches and picket lines make them uneasy. Even many of the Negroes' political supporters, including President Kennedy, opposed the March, believing it might impede passage of the civil rights legislation Kennedy had proposed. Thus the civil rights movement was confronted with three challenges. The first was simply to articulate its demands in a manner Americans could understand and approve. The second challenge was to overcome the reservations about protest tactics rooted in American culture, and the third was to win civil rights legislation.

In light of the lack of discipline and the confrontationism which marked the mass demonstrations that descended on Washington in the last few years, many are tempted to dismiss the 1963 March as an anomaly, a fluke, mere happenstance. But this explanation is superficial.

The March succeeded because it was the product of sound political philosophy and intelligent, responsible strategy. This meant a strict adherence to nonviolent principles. It also meant that the March's political program was broad enough to draw a positive response from the majority of Americans. Moreover, the March's program was not utopian; it could readily be translated into legislation. And, in fact, most of the ten demands that I spelled out before the Lincoln Memorial were subsequently enacted into law.[3]

3. The ten demands were: (1) comprehensive and effective civil rights legislation—without compromise or filibuster—to guarantee all Americans access to all public accommodations, decent housing, adequate and integrated education, and the right to vote; (2) the witholding of federal funds from all programs in which discrimination exists; (3) desegregation of all school districts in 1963; (4) enforcement of the Fourteenth Amendment and the reduction of congressional representation of states where citizens are disenfranchised; (5) a new executive order banning discrimination in all housing supported by federal funds; (6) authority for the attorney general to institute injunctive suits when any constitutional right is violated; (7) a massive federal program to train and place all unemployed workers—Negro and white—in meaningful and dignified jobs at decent

An important aspect of the March was its interracial character. Its program was addressed to poor and working-class whites, as well as to blacks, for it sought full employment, job training, an expanded housing program, and a substantial increase in the minimum wage. This program expanded the civil rights agenda by giving it a working-class perspective. In his address at the March, A. Philip Randolph proclaimed ". . . this civil rights revolution is not confined to the Negro, nor is it confined to civil rights, for our white allies know they cannot be free while we are not, and we know we have no future in a society in which six million black and white people are unemployed and millions live in poverty."

The March was, finally, an expression of the unity that existed both within the civil rights movement and within the broader liberal arena. With the exception of James Farmer, who sent a message from a Louisiana jail where he was incarcerated, every major civil rights leader was present at the March as were representatives from a broad spectrum of labor, liberal, and religious groups.[4]

If the March on Washington represented the high point of the era of protest, the 1964 Democratic National Convention, held less than a year after the March, marked its sym-

---

wages; (8) a national minimum wage act that will give all Americans a decent standard of living—government surveys show that anything less than $2.00 an hour fails to do this; (9) a broadened Fair Labor Standards Act to include all areas of employment that are presently excluded; (10) a federal Fair Employment Practices Act barring discrimination by federal, state, and municipal governments, and by employers, contractors, employment agencies, and trade unions.

4. Farmer and several hundred other demonstrators were jailed in Plaquemine, La., during a massive voter registration campaign.

bolic conclusion. That convention was highlighted by the challenge initiated by the Mississippi Freedom Democratic Party, a challenge with far-reaching implications for the future of the civil rights struggle.

For years Negroes had been striving to make their voices heard. They had provoked the political system to respond to injustices; they had been martyred so that others could achieve the dignity that is the inherent right of every man; they had marched, and sung, and prayed so that, failing all else, America would be moved into recognizing their plight. And finally, on an August afternoon in Washington, a crescendo of voices, 200,000 strong, had appealed to the nation for justice and dignity.

In all this, however, blacks had acted as outsiders to the political system. Their influence was felt, and their votes sought. But Negroes were not a part of the regular, normal process of government decision making. To include them in this process was not just morally right, it was politically necessary if there was to be a permanent, ongoing Negro movement that strived for basic economic change.

Our goal at the 1964 convention was to generate a movement that would become the dominant force within the Democratic party. The Republican party, having been captured by the Goldwaterites, was dismissed as a lost cause. The problem we faced was that the Democratic party, as it was then constituted, was a far cry from being the liberal mechanism we hoped to build. The South and the urban machine bosses no longer had the last word. But they were still effective instruments of conservatism, and in the case of the South, could still wield the power of the veto in racial matters. The South and the machines were not, of course, the social forces on which we anticipated building a more ideologically liberal party. We rather envisioned a party dominated by a coalition consisting of the labor movement, the minorities, and the liberals. We felt that such an alliance had the potential to win a majority simply because its various components possessed an ideological commitment to social change and a personal relationship to working people.

For some blacks, though, particularly those residing in the rural South, acquiring political power was of more urgency than building a coalition. In counties where blacks, although the majority, were governed by an oppressive white minority determined to keep blacks under its heel, it was essential that the black majority gain control of local political institutions. Clearly this was a matter of simple justice, although it would not, as some naively believed, bring about noticeable improvements in local economic conditions.

Thus the civil rights movement had to confront both immediate and long-range political goals. At Atlantic City we hoped to begin the long and difficult process of securing a leadership role within the political system. The most important thing in our minds at Atlantic City was to feel that we were making headway even if in realistic terms our gains were largely token. Seen in this context, I believe that the decision of the Freedom Democrats to spurn the compromise settlement was a strategic error. A victory of unprecedented scale had in fact been achieved. Not only were racist delegations dealt a setback, but of more consequence, racial discrimination was outlawed for future conventions. This arrangement would, in turn, set in motion a process that would open up the party machinery in state after state, would encourage more blacks to seek and win office, and would contribute to the eventual moderation of racial policies that had dominated the South for a century.

The rejection of the compromise settlement was not simply an isolated tactical mistake. In a broader sense, it reflected the agony that the civil rights movement was experiencing as it tried to come to grips with a situation with which, by tradition and training, it was unequipped to deal.

When Dr. King, Walter Reuther, and I spoke to the Freedom Democrats, urging them to accept the compromise, we stressed the point that the objectives of the civil rights movement were shifting from the legal to the economic and political. Confronted with a new agenda, we had to come to terms with the necessity of developing new tactics. When we had absolute demands for the rights of freedom and dignity, we could insist upon absolute solutions. But when you are working within the political system, you can no longer deal in absolute terms. You must be prepared to compromise, to make and accept concessions. You have to pay much more attention to how an issue is presented, and with what forces you align yourself. We also told the MFDP that as the representatives of a people who had been operating outside the political system, they had won a great victory. We proposed that they recognize this fact and move ahead, building on that triumph for even broader future gains.

The guiding force of the MFDP was the Student Non-Violent Coordinating Committee. A few years after the 1964 convention SNCC collapsed. Its grand design for transforming southern politics had failed. It found that it could not build a political movement consisting exclusively of poor people—sharecroppers, moreover, who until recently had not even been permitted to vote, much less develop any minimal level of political sophistication.

In pointing this out, I do not mean to appear overcritical of SNCC. Among its membership were some of the most intelligent and fearless political activists this nation has ever seen. That so many of them have dropped out of the racial struggle is one of the tragic consequences of our failure to resolve the problems which confronted the movement during its transition period.

SNCC's failure also reveals a problem which is rooted in the nature of American political parties. Unlike the parties in Europe, American parties have failed to impart to those outside the party framework—whether they be minorities, young people, or working people—a historical perspective, a reason for being. There is no ideological tradition which binds the disenfranchised to either party and, lacking this tradition, the alienated often seek political release outside the mainstream of party structure. Within the Democratic party, the party of the working man, there were only two forces which conveyed a sense of tradition from generation to generation. One was the South, with a long-standing history of keeping the Negro down. The other was the urban political machine, rooted for decades in the spoils system.

Thus while the Democrats were generally thought to favor programs that would effect social progress, the party had no sustaining vision of how this would be accomplished. On an ad hoc basis, the Democrats had a good record for supporting progressive measures. But they had little idea of the kind of society they wanted to build, and so their plans were carelessly conceived. The failure of the Democratic party to develop such a vision, or, if you will, class analysis, was to have dire consequences for the civil rights movement and, as we shall see, for the broader arena of liberalism as well.

# 3
# agenda
# for the
# future

With the passage of the Voting Rights Act in 1965, the civil rights movement entered a new period, which was to see the transformation of the Negro struggle from a movement that pursued social goals by means of mass protest into a movement that sought political objectives by means of traditional political methods. The transition from protest to politics was neither swift nor smooth. To many Americans, in fact, it appeared that the transition was not from protest to politics, but from nonviolent civil disobedience to violent disruption and rioting. The northern ghettoes seemed to explode with despair and hatred: thirty-four persons were killed in the 1965 Watts riot alone, while nearly one hundred died during the long hot summer of 1967, when riots erupted in the ghettoes of thirty-two cities.

Why had this come about? Americans, certainly American liberals, did not have the answer, at least not an answer that pointed to a realizable solution. The common liberal interpretation of the Kerner commission report on racial unrest was to blame the racist attitudes of individual whites for the lack of racial progress.[1] This attitude gave little con-

1. Officially known as the National Advisory Commission on Civil Disorders, the Kerner commission, chaired by Otto Kerner, the governor of Illinois, was established by President Johnson in the wake of widespread and bloody rioting during 1967. The report, issued in February, 1968, contained a harsh indictment of white racism and warned that America was becom-

sideration to the root cause of the discriminatory functioning of basic social and economic institutions. The favorable reception accorded the Kerner report was symptomatic of society's refusal to look beyond the superficial reflections of racial polarization. The Negro's supporters were obsessed with white guilt, whereas the conservative opponents of civil rights saw the mounting urban turmoil as a means of exploiting the law and order issue, which they did rather effectively in Richard Nixon's presidential campaign of 1968.

Lying beneath the rhetoric of conservatives and the self-flagellation of the Left was a series of complex and interrelated currents which, in combination with some serious strategical mistakes by the civil rights movement, radically altered the direction of the black struggle. Many of these changes were not the result of the failures of the civil rights movement; they were instead the natural outgrowth of its success.

By the end of 1965 the principal legislative objectives of what might be described as the initial black agenda—which dealt with the fabric of social and political discrimination in the southern states—had been achieved. But with success came the realization that a much more basic agenda was

---

ing two separate and unequal societies. The problem with the Kerner report was not so much in what it said, but in how its conclusions, particularly those relating to "white racism," were interpreted. Although the report was quite clear in urging basic social and economic reforms, many people took its message to imply that individual attitudes, rather than institutional structures, would have to be changed before the black person achieved an equal place in society. Thus, for many people advancing black progress became a matter of soul searching rather than social change.

still to be completed, one which would combat the fundamental inequalities built into the economic structure. That structure had to be changed if racial equality was to amount to anything more than a well-turned phrase. But, for a number of reasons, the forces comprising the leadership of the civil rights coalition were unequipped to cope with this new, broader agenda.

Chief among the problems thrust dramatically and often violently upon the consciousness of Americans in the mid-1960s was the increasing desperation of a vast slum proletariat in the northern ghettoes. The growth of this urban underclass, and its worsening condition of poverty and dislocation, did not come about through happenstance, but was the natural consequence of the direction of the economic system as well as the conscious policies of the federal government.

The creation of the northern ghetto resulted from two developments: the growth of agricultural technology, which made the use of massive numbers of sharecroppers and field hands obsolete in the South; and the expanding industrialization of the North. These developments reached their fruition in the period after World War II, when Negroes by the thousand migrated from the rural South to the industrialized North. What they found there, at least initially, were jobs.

In the period immediately following the war black unemployment dropped dramatically—to 4.1 percent in 1953, a figure lower than at any time before or after. The jobs filled by these black migrants, however, were almost entirely in the unskilled and semiskilled categories, those areas of the economy most susceptible to the ravages of automation and advanced technology. The acceleration of the technological revolution eliminated many jobs from central city areas at the same time that industries began moving from inner cities to the suburbs. Thus factory jobs in the cities were becoming scarcer while the expanding sectors of the economy often required a highly skilled or college-educated work force.

The late 1950s and, particularly, the 1960s, saw the consequence of rapidly changing manpower requirements, combined with the lack of national manpower and planning policies: there gradually emerged a massive army of unemployed or underemployed ghetto residents. The United States Department of Labor's 1967 study of "subemployment" in the urban slums suggests the depth of the ghetto's problems. The subemployment index, in addition to listing those "actively looking" but unable to find work, also estimates those who have dropped out of the labor market in despair, those who are working part-time but want full-time jobs, the working poor, and a conservatively estimated portion of males who are known to live in the slums, but who do not appear on any government employment records. In the ten cities surveyed, the subemployment rate for the inner city ghettoes stood at 35 percent. That is, more than one of every three employable adults was either unemployed or working for less than subsistence wages.

To the urban underclass, the civil rights revolution of which they had heard so much was a frustrating reminder of the plight of their daily lives. The initial impact of the protest movement had been limited to one geographical region—the South, where the consequences of the voting rights and civil rights acts were immediate and profound.

The northern black, however, saw only an ironic contrast between the proclamations of black progress, and the tangible conditions of his own life and environment. Far from improving, the status of ghetto life seemed to be rapidly deteriorating, as housing, transportation, health care, and education systems moved inexorably towards collapse.

Intensifying the bitterness of the underclass was another, largely unnoticed development: the emergence of a relatively prosperous middle and professional class which sought, as soon as was economically feasible, to flee the ghetto for white neighborhoods or for integrated or heavily black suburbs. I am not asserting, as some observers have, that the majority of blacks had reached the middle class—obviously they had not. A more accurate assessment would be that during the 1960s a majority of blacks had moved from the ranks of the impoverished into the broad working class, a development which in itself had profound implications. At the same time, it is a fact that for the first time a sizable number of young blacks were entering well-paid professions and that they, along with their creative resources and energy, were abandoning the slums for better neighborhoods. With their departure, a stabilizing element was removed from the structure of ghetto life, and this loss affected the black community's political fabric, the condition of its housing, its potentiality for organizing to demand improved city services, and of course, the already spiraling crime rate.

Aside from the demographic factors, we were confronted with other serious problems both within the civil rights movement and without, in the broader society's perception of the needs of black people.

1. The increasing social cost of black demands. One of the major reasons for the civil rights movement's initial success in mobilizing the support of a broad majority was that its initial agenda required little sacrifice from society; equal access to public facilities and voting rights were easily enough granted. The same was not true, however, when civil rights activists advanced broad proposals calling for full employment, manpower development, and the guarantee of adequate housing for all. When in 1966 A. Philip Randolph proposed the Freedom Budget, a ten-year plan to erase poverty, the *Wall Street Journal* commented: "It ought to be obvious that a useful effort to meet the problems of the relatively few Americans who are still in need requires a policy that shows promise of working, not simply for fresh outpourings of money from the Federal Government or anywhere else." The *Journal's* attitude was not untypical. Many congressmen used variations on the same theme in their attempts, often successful, to water down or emasculate antipoverty legislation. By cutting back on social expenditures, Congress was ensuring the failure of many promising efforts. What Leon Keyserling has as said of the federal housing program applies to many other programs that were oversold to the public and then underfunded by Congress:

> The reason why the effort to rehouse low income families has "failed" is that it has not been tried, except in token form. An annual building program averaging one-twentieth of the annual need has inevitably raised almost as many problems as it has solved. It has tended to make "poor houses" of the

public projects. It has permitted the slums
to remain in full force. It has perpetrated
one of the most dangerous of all social er-
rors, to offer promises rather than perfor-
mance.[2]

2. The diminishment of civil rights as a national priority.
For which, one should add, the liberals bear a heavy burden of responsibility. It was not, as some would have it,
simply the intensification of the Vietnam War that turned
the nation's attention from racial problems. Race issues and
the broader question of abolishing poverty have been replaced by many concerns other than the war: women's lib-
eration, the environment, and political corruption, to name
a few. Nor was it that the needs of black people were any
less acute. Indeed, having raised the expectations of black
people, it was now more important than ever for America to
follow through on its promises of a just society. The problem was that racial equality proved a much more difficult
problem to solve than anyone had ever anticipated. And for
those whose commitment to the black cause was less than
total, the demands were too great. It was far easier for them
to move on to another issue.

A social movement, if its imprint is to be permanent and
transforming, must have an economic base. Moral fervor
cannot maintain it, nor can the act of participation itself.
There must be a genuine commitment to the advancement
of poor and working people. To have such a commitment is
also to have a militant sense of responsibility, a recognition

2. Leon Keyserling, *The Coming Crisis in Housing* (Washington, D.C.: Conference on Economic Progress, 1972), p. 42.

that actions have consequences which have very real effects on the individual lives of those whom one seeks to advance. Far too many current movements lack both an economic perspective and a sense of responsibility, and they fail because of it.

The failures of many of the new political movements are not necessarily the fault of the participants. These people are guilty simply of having accepted the myth that America is a classless, "affluent" society. The rediscovery of poverty was not brought about by an increase in the number of poor. It was the result of the incessant prodding of black people who, of course, constitute a substantial percentage of the poor.

The recognition of poverty did little, however, to alter fundamentally the long-held belief in the convergence of the working and middle classes. America was willing to admit to the existence of widespread poverty. But the nation was not prepared to acknowledge that working Americans suffered from severe problems, that those problems were measurably different from those of the middle class, and that the problems of working Americans deserved attention from the government.

3. The fragmentation of the civil rights movement. Whites are wrong to believe that all blacks think monolithically and share common social and economic roots. There is class consciousness among blacks just as there is among whites, and nothing demonstrates this fact more clearly than the divergent paths taken by the once unified civil rights movement. This is not to deny that there was a superficial unity within the black community while the main target was Jim Crow. Segregation, after all, was an institu-

tion which affected the businessman just as it affected the sharecropper. But the new civil rights laws did not benefit all classes equally. The black middle class had the financial resources to take advantage of its newly achieved rights and these laws significantly enhanced its social mobility. For the poor, the benefits were far less tangible and much more psychological.

There are those who deplored the lack of unity among the recognized black leadership. I do not believe, however, that black disunity was a significant cause of the problems the civil rights movement encountered.

The very concept of black unity is illusory, raising expectations that can never be fulfilled and diverting the attention of society from more substantive issues. In a pluralistic democracy, racial unity is a meaningless goal. It is far more important for blacks to form alliances with other forces in society which share common needs and common goals, and which are in general agreement over the means to achieve them. It is pointless to talk of unity between Roy Wilkins, who advocates integration, and Roy Innis, who wants to resegregate black schools. Nor does it make sense to pursue unity between blacks who favor national health insurance and a black medical association that opposes it.

4. The differences over tactics and strategy within the black community. One must recall that the almost total unity of black leadership had been the cutting edge of the March on Washington; then the black community had spoken as one, thus removing any lingering ambiguity about what the black man wanted from society. But the strong consensus that was achieved—not without considerable difficulty—in 1963 could not reasonably have been expected to

persist when the goals of the movement evolved from the juridical to the political and economic. This evolution was a natural and in some ways a healthy development, for it provoked within the black community an important debate over future tactics, future coalitions, and future objectives.

While there are few outright conservatives in the black community, there have always been differing political outlooks. Two of the most influential black leaders, A. Philip Randolph and Whitney Young, held radically divergent views about the social force with which blacks should align themselves. Young felt that the enlightened segments of the business community would make the most significant contribution to the economic progress of the black masses, whereas Randolph believed passionately that the labor movement and its program would ultimately be responsible for bringing blacks into the economic mainstream. Others, of course, held less traditional views. There was a growing separatist movement which, although it exerted little influence on the masses of black workers, attained status through the publicity it generated in the media. There were those who felt that community organizing and the grassroots participation of the poor would give the alienated underclass a strong voice in the decisions shaping its destiny. And there was even the miniscule, but well-publicized, fraction which celebrated the use of violence as a means of achieving freedom through revolution.

The differences within the black community reflected the divisions that had erupted between the traditional allies of racial progress in the liberal and labor arenas. These divisions cut across a broad series of issues, ranging from those relating to specific policy to differences relating to the fundamental outlook on society and the role of the state.

One specific consequence of these divisions was the weakening of the Great Society's impact. I do not share the prevalent view that President Johnson's domestic initiatives amounted to nothing more than ambitious failure. The Great Society did, in fact, trigger a national response to the plight of the poor and minority groups that was both psychological and real. The concept of improving social services for the poor through the injection of federal funds was a sound one, particularly when combined with policies to stimulate economic growth and employment. And one of the most widely criticized Great Society enterprises, manpower training, was among its most important innovations; it was geared to meet the urgent social need of retraining workers who would otherwise be consigned to a lifetime of dead-end jobs.

But there were serious problems with the Johnson administration's strategy as well as some tragically missed opportunities. These problems were partially due to Johnson's view of himself as a "consensus" politician, a leader who could move the country ahead without challenging any of the predominant social forces. Thus, instead of directly opposing the inherent tendency of capitalism to discourage full employment, Johnson relied on the civic-mindedness of the business community to stimulate the hiring of more blacks and implement manpower-training endeavors. We soon discovered that social revolutions of the magnitude that Johnson proposed are not achieved through tax credits to industries or voluntary hiring programs.

Nor are the answers to the problems of the poor to be found in formulas that encourage their "participation," however important that might be. Underlying the community-action strategy was the profoundly flawed assumption that there is something inherently wrong with the poor, with their pattern of social dislocation or whatever, and that it is this "wrongness," rather than the basic reality of the way in which the economic system functions, that perpetuates their state of deprivation. Acting on this assumption, the Johnson administration proceeded to set up a series of programs to enable the poor to organize themselves better, believing that somehow the poor could organize themselves out of poverty. To be sure, the poverty program did have its value, but it was a poor substitute for programs which could put the unemployed to work, or could assist the underemployed into better-paying, more satisfying jobs. In addition, the community-action approach was diversionary. It deluded people into believing that broad economic change could be accomplished through picket lines at city hall or through rent strikes. Also, it lessened support for the antipoverty effort among those politicians who resented the disruptions generated by some of the community-action agencies.

It is clear now that the Johnson administration might well have succeeded had it concentrated the bulk of its funds and energies on one objective: ensuring a job for everyone. To institutionalize a full-employment policy would have been a radical step—one which, no doubt, would have eroded Johnson's consensus of support within the business community. But such a step would have attacked poverty at the root while appealing to the broad majority of Americans who, no matter what their conservative instincts might be, have time and again indicated that they would support a program to bring about full employment.

The controversy over community-action strategy was but one reflection of a much deeper problem: the tendency to substitute psychological strategies for economic solutions to the poverty problem. The problem of black identity—of how the black man relates to and asserts himself in an often hostile, predominantly white world—cannot be minimized. The role of the American Negro has been a terribly difficult one, far more difficult than that of the ethnic immigrant who could at least identify with a native homeland and at the same time merge without serious difficulty into the pattern of American life. Blacks, on the other hand, had a dual struggle: to achieve recognition as free and equal human beings and to enter the mainstream of American life, being accepted, without discrimination, as equal competitors.

A half century ago, W. E. B. DuBois wrote of this problem eloquently in his monumental work *The Souls of Black Folk:*

> After the Egyptian and Indian, the Greek and Roman, the Teuton and Mongolian, the Negro is a sort of seventh son, born with a veil, and gifted with second sight in this American world—a world which yields him no true self-consciousness but only lets himself see himself through the revelation of the other world. It is a peculiar feeling, this double consciousness, this sense of always looking at one's self through the eyes of others, of measuring one's soul by the tape of a

world that looks on in amused contempt and pity. One ever feels his twoness—an American, a Negro; two souls, two thoughts, two unreconciled strivings; two warring ideals in one dark body, whose dogged strength alone keeps it from being torn asunder.

The history of the American Negro is the history of this strife—the longing to attain this self-conscious manhood, to merge his double self into a truer and better self. In this merging he wishes neither of the older selves to be lost. He would not Africanize America, for America has too much to teach Africa and the world. He would not bleach his Negro soul in a flood of white Americanism, for he knows that Negro blood has a message for the world. He simply wishes to make it possible for a man to be both a Negro and an American, without being cursed and spit upon by his fellows, without having the doors of opportunity closed roughly in his face.[3]

If what DuBois wrote was true for his generation, it is even more relevant for the modern Negro, the Negro of the post-civil rights era. It has often been observed that freedom is a much more difficult state to cope with than are conditions of bondage or oppression. And while no black

3. W. E. B. DuBois, *The Souls of Black Folk* (Greenwich, Conn.: Fawcett, 1961), pp. 16–17.

person would choose to return to segregation and inferior social condition, few would deny the reality of the trauma which accompanied the newly won liberties.

The reflections of the problem of dual consciousness were widespread. Perhaps the most characteristic was the controversy over what the Negro should be called: Negro, black, Afro-American, even African-American. Blacks could not simply call themselves Americans, since no matter how significant their progress, they were not accepted as full participants in society, race consciousness still being a disturbingly prominent fact of life.

It should be noted that the striving for group identity is not a phenomenon limited to black Americans. In the United States, the debate over assimilation versus separatism, the melting pot as against highly competitive pluralism, has been taken up by Indians, Hispanics, ethnic immigrant groups, even women. Outside the United States, any number of groups—Irish, Scots, Welsh, Walloons, Basques, Croatians, Russian Jews, the Ibos of Biafra, black non-Moslems of the Sudan—have experienced the same dual struggle for group identity in a context of social acceptance by the dominant society.

American blacks now need to realize that there is a difference between viewing racial pride as a positive psychological attribute and attempting to build a social policy based on racialism. It is, in fact, impossible to forge a creative, long-term social agenda based on racial, ethnic, or sexual goals. To attempt such an agenda is self-defeating and reactionary and will ultimately impede the advancement both of society and of a particular group itself.

Thus it is hardly surprising to hear the proposal of a black separatist, such as Roy Innis, echoed by Richard Nixon, or to read that Innis's proposals to resegregate black schools found favor with Lester Maddox and George Wallace. Innis's rhetoric may sound militant, but his program appeals to the most conservative forces in society, particularly to those who are the most strongly opposed to government intervention in the the nation's economic and social fabric. The only "civil rights" program for which the Nixon administration displayed a measure of enthusiasm was black capitalism, the least effective and the least challenging to the status quo.

These observations reveal a basic problem that confronted the civil rights movement in the mid-1960s: the separatist impulse emerged precisely when the need for a new and sophisticated approach to coalition politics was greatest. During the period when nonviolent protest was the major weapon of civil rights forces, the role of whites was peripheral to the black struggle. Their moral support and volunteer assistance were welcomed, but their participation in sit-ins, boycotts, and voter-registration drives did not determine the success of these endeavors. Ordinary black people served as the moral force which elicited concession after concession from the South and won the respect and support of the rest of the nation.

The achievement of protest's initial objectives, however, brought a significant change to the basic character of the civil rights agenda. What had previously been a movement seeking exclusively racial goals was now called upon to challenge the fundamental class nature of the economic structure. To be sure, the majority of civil rights leaders, except for the most extreme and ineffectual militants, did not define their goals in terms of class struggle. Nonetheless, the very fact that certain fundamental issues were raised—the discriminatory workings of the housing market, full employment as a basic human right, the equalization of public funds for educational purposes, free medical care for those in need—implied a substantial assault on the traditional workings of the nation's economic structure and thus on its class structure as well.

It has become commonplace to dismiss the concept of political coalition as outmoded, unworkable, and incapable of meeting the unique needs of newly liberated groups. Blacks, ethnic groups, women—those whose personal and political aspirations have in the past been systematically suppressed by the dominant white society must, we are told, assert their rights as interest groups, or as causes, rather than as members of a broader alliance of political forces; otherwise their special needs will be subordinated to the program of the majority, a program which, some say, will eventually reveal itself to be antagonistic to that of the minority.

There is no question that coalition politics is a complex phenomenon. A successful liberal political alliance is enormously difficult to build and, once pieced together, even more difficult to maintain, given the inevitable tensions, rivalries, and antagonisms of the various partners. The most successful recent liberal coalition, that which carried Lyndon B. Johnson to the presidency in 1964, achieved its almost Gaullist proportions only because of the imminent dangers posed by the Goldwater candidacy.

But if the forging of a political alliance is a formidable proposition, it is still a necessary one. Blacks in particular cannot afford go-it-alone strategies. Every time they have resorted to separatist schemes, they have been doomed to abysmal failure. Blacks must have allies who share common problems and pursue common goals. The challenge is to choose the right allies, not simplistically, or in a superficial, consensus way, but on the basis of their specific programs and proven willingness to cooperate with a political partner.

The attitude of separatist-minded blacks was not the only factor complicating the building of a coalition broad enough to accomplish the ambitious program of economic reform that comprised the new civil rights agenda. Far more important, in fact, were the mounting divisions within the liberal community, the growing disillusionment of intellectuals with the Great Society, and the outright hostility of some liberals to the labor movement. The most devastating consequence of the crisis of liberalism was, of course, the defeat of Hubert Humphrey for the presidency in 1968, a defeat that was sealed by the refusal of some liberals to support the vice-president and the lukewarm support accorded him by others. If nothing else, this election demonstrated that members of the New Politics segment of the Democratic party has lost that sense of priority which had guided them to victory in 1964. To them the well-being of black people was no longer a prime consideration. They were willing to sacrifice the goals of racial progress to what they discerned as more pressing concerns: ending the Vietnam War (which Humphrey would most likely have accomplished much faster and in a much more humanitarian manner than did Nixon) and their own drive for ascendancy within the Democratic party.

The discontent of liberals with coalition politics also had important legislative ramifications. In 1966 a number of liberals closely identified with the peace movement refused to endorse A. Philip Randolph's Freedom Budget because of its failure to demand massive cutbacks in defense spending.[4] Some went so far as to declare that poverty could be abolished without increased economic growth or an infusion of additional federal funds. The poverty problem, they insisted, would be resolved once the war had ended and the so-called peace dividend—monies that had been channeled into war expenditures and could subsequently be used for domestic projects—became available. The peace windfall never materialized, of course, and its proponents' only achievement was to divert the attention of American society away from its most urgent concerns: the need for a fundamental change in the tax structure, accelerated economic growth, and a renewed commitment to the original priorities of the Great Society—more and better housing, manpower, development, compensatory education, federal financing of health care, and the like.

In addition to the slippage of liberal faith in the Great Society, we witnessed a growing liberal hostility toward organized labor. Labor was seen not as a progressive force, but as a reactionary and racist institution, with a bigoted membership and a leadership devoid of social vision. The causes of this hostile attitude were many and complex: class bias and snobbery, a lack of understanding of labor's goals

4. Randolph's Freedom Budget was a ten-year program to abolish poverty, stressing a full-production economy and massive infusions of federal funds to housing, health care, education, jobs, environmental control, etc. A broad coalition of labor, civil rights, liberal and religious figures endorsed the Freedom Budget concept.

and accomplishments, and an as-yet-unarticulated desire to supplant the labor movement's position within the Democratic party.

The effects of the changed liberal attitude were clearly to give comfort to the conservative, traditionally antilabor forces at the very moment when the interests of labor were dovetailing with those of the black community. Indeed, black people now had an increasing stake in the strength of organized labor, for black workers were entering heavily unionized fields in substantially higher proportion than were white workers. To weaken labor would, of course, harm the interests of these workers and of all workers who would enter the labor movement in the future. More important, however, was the political role occupied by labor. The AFL-CIO, UAW, and other unions comprised the vanguard in the struggle to extend racial gains beyond the juridical. The progressive leadership provided by the labor movement became crucial after the election of Richard Nixon, as labor assumed a pivotal role in the numerous campaigns to beat back the new administration's anti-civil rights initiatives. Indeed, blacks discovered that labor was the only significant social force which could be depended upon to press the safeguarding of the social and economic rights achieved through protest and struggle.

There is an increasing awareness that the future of black Americans is inextricably tied to the future of America itself. Indeed, the most significant achievement of the civil rights struggle has been to transform blacks from a separate and inferior class into a group that has entered the mainstream, not fully or as equals yet, but as a group which nonetheless has a vital stake in the direction of our state and culture.

We have now learned that everything which moves and shapes society moves and shapes black people as well. If government policies weaken the economy, stifle economic growth, and contribute to massive unemployment, black people suffer ever more severely than in those days past when they had little connection with the economic mainstream, when the southern black sharecropper and the domestic worker comprised a large percentage of the black work force. Black people are no longer marginally attached to the economy, the political system, and the overall culture. They are actively affecting and affected by these institutions. When blacks were relegated to underfinanced segregated schools, and systematically excluded from opportunities for higher learning, the success or failure of American education was a small issue in their day-to-day struggle for survival. Today the foundations of segregation have been destroyed; the doors of colleges and universities have opened for minority students; and education has assumed a much more pivotal role for entry into society. And if, as seems to be the case today, society begins to undermine the value of public education, it is blacks who suffer most severely.

But while blacks have become participants in American society, we must not forget that they have not achieved full integration into our social and economic systems. The achievement of this integration constitutes the agenda of the future. But we must take care to learn from the experiences of the past. If blacks are now part of the system, they have a new responsibility to strengthen and democratize social institutions rather than to tear them down. This responsibility entails a continuing struggle against our traditional enemies—those who have a stake in the status quo and in reinforcing current inequalities. But we will also find ourselves pitted against new enemies—those who may once have been our allies, but whose priorities are ultimately antagonistic to the broad needs of underprivileged and working people.

Our foremost challenge is to keep the issue of economic change before the American people. The civil rights movement has won many of its social objectives, and we can be rightfully optimistic over finding long-range solutions for those problems remaining. But the issue of economic democracy confronts us still. The struggle to achieve a more humane economic order will not be fought along racial lines but will be defined by broader class realities. The degree to which this struggle is won will determine whether the goals for which so many in the civil rights movement sacrificed and died will be fulfilled in their entirety, or whether the high hopes which galvanized this profoundly important movement will lie half-realized.

# index